The **50** Best
Indoor Games
for Groups

The 50 Best Group Games Pocket Books

The 50 Best Games for Building Self-Esteem
The 50 Best Games for Sensory Perception
The 50 Best Games for Brain Exercise
The 50 Best Games for Relaxation & Concentration
The 50 Best Games for Speech & Language Development
The 50 Best Games for Children's Groups
The 50 Best Games for Groups
The 50 Best Indoor Games for Groups

The **50** Best
Indoor Games
for Groups

Josef Griesbeck
translated by Lilo Seelos

HINTON**HOUSE**

Published by

Hinton House Publishers Ltd
Newman House, 4 High Street,
Buckingham, MK18 1NT, UK

info@hintonpublishers.com
www.hintonpublishers.com

First published 2009
Reprinted 2012

Printed in the United Kingdom by Hobbs the Printers Ltd

British Library Cataloguing in Publication Data
Griesbeck, Josef.
    The 50 best indoor games for groups. – (The 50 best group games
    pocket books ; 8)
    1. Indoor games. 2. Group games
    I. Title II. Series III. Fifty best games for rainy days
    793-dc22

    ISBN-13: 9781906531157

Originally published in German by Don Bosco
Verlag München under the title *Die 50 besten*
Regenwetterspiele © Don Bosco Verlag, München 2005

FSC
www.fsc.org
MIX
Paper from
responsible sources
FSC® C020438

Contents

Contents

'A person who no longer has
fun is no fun to be with.'

– Edmund Johannes Lutz

Who Am I?

This game is suitable for initial sessions and also for when group members don't know each other very well.

Ideally, everyone should sit in a circle for this game. Explain the rules to the group, and then give everyone a little time to try to memorise the others.

Now, choose someone to start and ask everyone else to close their eyes. That person must describe one of the other group members. Once people think they know who is being described, keeping their eyes closed, they must point in the direction they think the person is sitting.

Simple version

☼ 'The person I am thinking of is wearing jeans and has long hair. She's got white socks on …'

More difficult version

(For when the group know each other a little better.)

☼ The person I am thinking of likes to laugh a lot. She is always on time…'

A Rose for Ruth

Names are very important to people, so people's names should be recognised and used with respect. Once in a while, however, it is OK to play with people's names.

Game 1

Ask the group to think of objects and words that they like which begin with the same initial letter as their names. For example, Ruth might think of: 'rose, rain, Rome, rabbit, raspberry, red …'. She can then share her ideas with the group.

Game 2

Ask the group to sit in a circle and think of words that start with 'R' which, in their view, suit Ruth.

Anonymous Calling Cards

Give each person a pen and piece of paper or card. Now ask the group to find a quiet space for themselves by spreading out around the room.

Give them a few minutes to write their own 'Calling Card'. To do this, each person must write down as many facts about themselves as possible, using short, simple sentences without writing down their name or any obvious descriptive details (e.g., blond hair, glasses).

Instead, encourage people to think of statements such as 'I'm nearly always hungry – I wear contact lenses – I have a really impressive scar from an appendix operation – I am desperate to visit America' and so on. They should try to aim for at least five statements but between eight and twelve would be better.

Variation 1

This activity is suitable for smaller groups. Display all of the 'Anonymous Calling Cards' on the walls. Ask the group to walk around the room and try to guess who the cards might refer to. Cards could be numbered and answers written on sheets.

Variation 2

The 'Calling Cards' can be folded, put in a box and shuffled. Now every member of the group can draw a card and try to find out who it belongs to by asking yes/no questions.

This can either be done one at a time or with everyone playing at once. If someone guesses who a card belongs to, they can put the card back into the box and draw a new one.

Portraits

All of the group members sit in a circle and are each given an A5-sized piece of card and a coloured pen. If available, everyone could be given a small mirror.

Now each person must draw a self-portrait of their own face. They should try and make the portrait as accurate as possible.

As some people might find this rather daunting, try and use some humour in your instructions, for example, 'Don't forget to draw your sleepy eyes!'

Without showing anyone else, finished portaits should now be placed in a basket or box. The pictures are then shuffled before people try to guess who the individual portraits belong to.

Variations

- ☼ Group members could draw caricatures of themselves instead of portraits.

- ☼ A large sheet of paper or an old piece of wallpaper is placed on the floor for each person in the group. One person lies down on the paper while someone else traces around them to draw their outline.

- ☼ Each person in the group could bring in a baby picture of themselves.

City Breaks

The whole group sit on chairs in a circle.

One by one each person names a city from anywhere in the world – perhaps somewhere they have been on holiday, or a place they have always wanted to visit. If the group is quite large, they might like to go around the circle a couple of times to make sure everyone is familiar with all the different city names.

Choose one player to start, they now stand in the middle of the circle and name two of the cities by announcing: 'I'm travelling from London to Miami.' The two members of the groups whose cities have been named have to swap places. While they do so, the person in the middle has to try to grab one of the empty chairs. The person left standing chooses the next two cities.

Variation

You could introduce levels of complication by naming more than two cities at a time, for example, 'I'm travelling from London to Miami, via Vienna and Madrid'.

Forbidden Words

In this game, players must hold conversations but are not allowed to use certain words. Decide among the group which words are forbidden, an easy way to start is with 'yes' and 'no'.

All players walk around the room and at a signal from you choose a partner and engage in conversation. They are allowed to say anything except the words 'yes' and 'no'. So, if someone is asked, for example, 'Do you like animals?' they can't respond by saying, 'Yes, I do', but have to say something like, 'Not all of them'.

If a forbidden word is used during a conversation between two players, they have to split up and each find a new partner.

Stored Data

The group sit in a circle and take it in turns to say something they know about a chosen person, for example, Kirsten.

William says: 'I know that you have three brothers and sisters.'
Richard says: 'I know that you are a good chess player.'
Melanie says: 'I know that you have an uncle in Birmingham, who you like a lot.'

Kirsten's task is to give a counter or token to anyone whose statement is correct. When the whole group has had a turn, the round can start again until everyone in the circle has run out of things to say about Kirsten. If someone can't think of anything to say they are 'out'.

Players are not allowed to say things that are obvious, for example, 'I know that you have short hair', and are only allowed to make one statement at a time.

Now the game continues with another person. The winner is the player who has the most counters or tokens at the end of the game.

Me, Myself & My Dog

This game works best if the group has already met a few times and people are familiar with each other as they will feel more comfortable talking about themselves.

The game introduces the idea of an unfamiliar narrator. What would something that I own or use have to say about me?

Explain how the game works and allow the group some preparation time. Players should be given sufficient time to ask themselves the question without being distracted or interrupted.

People should choose something that could say a lot about them, for example, their dog, their bicycle, their school bag, and so on. If anyone wants to, they can make notes, but usually this is not necessary.

Once everyone has had enough time to think about what they are going to say, the story telling can begin, either within the whole group or smaller ones.

For example:
'The other day, my dog really complained about me. It only had one good thing to say, which I'll tell you now ...'

Variation

Stories can be written down and collected in, then shuffled and handed out again amongst the participants. They are then read out one at a time and people have to guess who they refer to.

Picture My Name

Give each person in the group a piece of paper or card and ask them to illustrate a picture sign for their name.

Instead of writing their names on the signs, group members must think of an object that starts with each letter of their name and draw these instead.

The resulting artwork can be displayed on the wall or the door of the group's meeting room. Pictures could be left 'in code' for others to guess or solutions printed underneath.

Crossword Names

Place a large piece of paper (e.g., a sheet from a flipchart or an old piece of wallpaper) on the floor. Depending on the age of the group, you may need to draw the outline boxes for a crossword puzzle.

One player starts by writing their first name either vertically or horizontally on the piece of paper. A second person adds their name by linking it with one of the letters of the first player's name.

Play continues until everyone has had a turn and a crossword of names has been created.

Variations

If there is room players could now enter other information about themselves that they feel is important. The game works best if the group agrees on a theme for each round, for example, 'Our places of birth', 'The streets where we live', 'Our favourite colours', and so on. A new crossword could be created for each theme and displayed on the wall.

Winning Numbers

This game requires preparation of number cards, which the players have to combine to create sums.

Give each person a number card, or ask them to draw a card from a hat. Their number should be kept secret until the game starts.

The aim of the game is to combine cards to make a given number, for example, 100. This means people need to find others whose cards will combine with theirs to make 100. The first group to reach 100 are the winners. There is no limit to the number of people in a group, as long as their cards add up to the correct number.

Example

Player 1 draws the number 20.

Player 2 draws the number 5.

Player 3 draws the number 85.

Player 4 draws the number 30.

Player 5 draws the number 60.

Player 6 draws the number 55.

Player 7 draws the number 10.

In this case, it is possible to combine the numbers in several ways to reach 100 (30+60+10 or 5+85+10 or 5+30+55+10). Which players will find each other first?

/... continued

Variations

You can make this game as easy or complicated as you like.

For example, you could choose odd number such as 31 or you could select a really big number such as 500 to be the winning number. Players may need to add, subtract or multiply to reach the desired number.

Hand Lotto

Between five and ten players sit together in a circle. Each person takes five objects from a selection of small items such as dried peas, matches or marbles that have been laid out in the middle of the table.

Now each player has to decide how many items they are going to place in their left hands. They must do this behind their backs or under the table, out of view of the other players. Any remaining items should be hidden or put into a pocket.

Then the big lotto number draw begins. The question players must answer is: 'What will be the total number of objects that the group members are holding in their left hands?'

Everyone writes down their guess on a piece of paper and these are collected by the group leader. Once everyone has written down their guess, all players open their left hands to show how many objects they are holding. The prize goes to the person who has guessed the correct total number of objects or is the closest.

The Correct Guess

This is the perfect game for a large number of players, because everyone can participate. Each player writes down their name on a piece of paper as well as a number indicating how many people they think it would take to join hands in order to surround the room or even the playground.

Now put the players' guesses to the test – the person who has guessed correctly or is closest to the correct number is the winner.

Variations

☼ How many potatoes will need to be peeled to feed everyone at lunch time? (Ask kitchen staff to keep count!)

☼ How many steps is it from the classroom to the playground?

The Coin Game

For this game you will need to place a number of different coins into a container.

One player starts by giving the container a good shake and then tipping the coins out onto the table.

Working with the other players if necessary, they must then add up the value of only those coins that have landed number-side up on the table. Each player gets a turn at shaking the container and adding up the value of their coins.

The winner is the person whose shake produces the largest sum.

Think of a Word

Give each person a pen and piece of paper. Ask everyone to write five letters on their piece of paper.

Now ask the group to divide into pairs and to combine the letters they have written on their sheets.

Once the pairs are settled, they have three minutes to make as many words as possible using only the 10 letters they have between them. Letters cannot be used twice unless they appear twice on the list.

When the time is up compare the lists of words – the pair with the most words is the winner.

☼ What influences the number of words produced?

☼ Can choosing certain letters change the outcome?

Object Pick-a-Stick

Ask the group to quickly collect together a large selection of everyday objects such as a comb, a key, a pencil, a clothes hanger or a brush, and pile them up in the middle of the table.

Then play starts following the usual Pick-a-Stick rules. The first player is allowed remove items from the pile until doing so causes one of the other objects to move. This must be carefully monitored by the other players. If an object moves, it is the next player's turn.

The winner is the player who has the most objects at the end of the game.

16

Circus

Originally the circus was an arena for competitions and games. The word 'circus' originates from the term 'circle'. This game is about having fun playing a circle circus game.

Players divide into at least two groups consisting of a maximum of eight people. They then sit back to back on two rows of chairs.

The first players on each row are the ringmasters, the people next to them are the trapeze artists, next are the animal trainers and finally the clowns. These people represent the circus family. They are joined in fifth place by the elephants, the horses, the lions and finally the snakes. This group represents the circus animals.

Now read out the Circus Story. Every time one of the characters is named, the corresponding player from the each group must get up and walk around the chairs in a circle, the player on the left walks around anticlockwise, the player on the right walks around clockwise.

If players hear 'circus family', all circus family players have to walk around simultaneously and if 'circus animals' is mentioned, all the 'animals' get a turn to walk around in a circle. The group whose player is last to arrive back at their place is given a minus point – however, running is not allowed! It might be wise to employ a non-playing 'circus secretary', who is in charge of noting down each group's points.

The Circus Story

(* indicates that someone has to walk around)

Today, a famous circus is coming to town. The ringmaster (*) is standing at the entrance to the exercise area looking at all his circus animals (*). He is pleased with the animal handling skills of his animal trainer (*), who is rehearsing a number with the horses (*). The clown (*) is sitting by the entrance, having a chat with the trapeze artist (*), who is keeping an eye on the restless lions (*) and snakes (*). Something doesn't seem to be quite right. The ringmaster (*) also senses this and is now watching the elephants (*) more closely. All of a sudden, the trapeze artist (*) lets out a huge scream and announces that the snakes (*) have escaped. The whole circus family (*) sets off to look for the snakes (*). The animal trainer (*) runs outside, the trapeze artist (*) searches the audience area, the clown (*) checks the other circus animals (*) and the ringmaster (*) supervises and gives instructions. But no one in the circus family (*) can find the snakes (*). The elephants (*) and the lions (*) are wondering why the whole circus family (*) is rushing about and, while the horses (*) are kicking the ground with their hooves, the first snake (*) slithers out of the straw. All the circus animals (*) start to panic, but the clown (*) manages to calm the whole circus family (*) down again.

Human Connect-Three

Most children know how to play 'Noughts & Crosses' or 'Connect Four'. This is a variation of these games and allows six players to play at once.

First, the group leader must mark out on the floor a square made up of three by three spaces. Then the players are divided into two teams, each team is given three cards numbered 1 to 3. It may help to have different coloured sets of cards, e.g., red and green.

The team members now line up facing each other on either side of the square, each holding their card.

Play starts with red card number one moving into one space, then green player one moves, then red player two, then green player two, and so on. The game continues with players from the different teams taking turns. The team members must move in the order of the numbers they are holding.

The aim of the game is for one team to manage to connect in a line either horizontally or diagonally next to each other. Players must always take their turn to move, even if this means that the opposing team will be able to connect three on their next move.

Zero Wins

For this game, each player will need a pen and a piece of paper. In addition, you will also need one or more dice.

The players start by each drawing 70 lines on their piece of paper. Now they take it in turns to roll the dice and must cross out the corresponding number of lines on their piece of paper.

This game becomes really exciting towards the end, as, in order to win the game, a player must to roll the exact number corresponding to the number of lines left on their piece of paper.

The winner is the player who is first to cross out all their lines.

Variations

The end of the game could be made more complex by a player having to add the difference between the number on the die and the number of lines left on their paper to the bottom of their page.

Dice Race

You will need two dice to play this game. All the players sit around the table, with the two dice placed in the middle.

At a signal, two players who are sitting opposite each other each start rolling one of the dice. As soon as they have rolled a six the players are allowed to pass the dice on to the player on their left. That person then also needs to roll a six before they too can pass the dice on, and so on.

Eventually it is likely that one player will end up with both dice at the same time. That player is out. Then the dice are placed in the middle again to start the next second round.

Variation

This game could be played in small groups as a race with just a single die – the first group to each roll a six is the winner!

Long-Johns are Best!

Two or more players stand opposite each other. The players on one side must give a speech raving about the virtues of pants and ranting against the wearing of long-johns. The person standing opposite them must do exactly the reverse. Set a time for the speeches and the group can vote on the most creative content.

This game is particularly suitable for playing in a circle, especially when the group's mood has reached a high and they need to let off steam.

21

Story Riddles

In this game the group are given a riddle and they must ask questions to uncover the background and so solve the riddle. However, they are only allowed to ask questions that can be answered with 'yes' or 'no'.

Example

A man lives on the 24th floor and uses the lift every day. In the morning, he gets in the lift on the 24th floor and gets out on the ground floor. When he comes back from work in the evening, he gets into the lift on the ground floor, but then gets out on the 15th floor and then uses the stairs to walk up to the 24th floor, where he lives. However, if it is raining, he always takes the lift all the way up to the 24th floor. Why?

Answer: The man is very short. When it rains, he carries an umbrella and uses it to reach the button for the 24th floor.

Double Meanings

Many words in the English language have more than one meaning, e.g., row, invalid, minute. If words are spelled the same but have different meanings, they are called homographs. If they sound the same but have different meanings, e.g., sea/see, wait/weight, they are called homophones.

Groups can have a lot of fun looking for such words.

There are also variations on this type of word search activity.

Example 1

Look for words or word combinations that contain numbers: L(one)ly, w(eight), of(ten)…

Example 2

Look for words that contain personal pronouns: (He)llo, (she)ep, (her)on, t(his), weat(her), (you)th …

Blind Painting

You may have heard about pictures that have been painted by blind people. Anyone can experience what it is like to paint without being able to see just by wearing a blindfold.

This might feel strange initially, but as people relax into the activity, their confidence will increase and very often great pieces of art can be created. Blindfold painting can be great fun!

Afterwards people can present their artwork to the group and discuss their experience of painting blindfolded.

Variations

Everyone could try to reproduce a familiar picture, or you could provide different themes for your painters, which could be sensible or even nonsense:

☼ A spaceship meets rainbow

☼ A bird collides with a plane

☼ A car on the moon

☼ Animals at the zoo

All About You

This game is best suited to situations where people are going to spend some time together.

To begin, each person writes their name on a piece of paper, folds it and puts it in a basket. After the pieces of paper have been shuffled, everyone selects one, this will be their target person. The chosen names must be kept secret and papers destroyed once read.

For the rest of their time together, the group members must find out as much as possible about the person whose name they have drawn, for example, by watching them carefully and by paying extra attention to what they have to say - all without the other person noticing.

At the end of their time together, the group can gather together to report. Each person must address the group as if they are the target person, using all the information they have gathered, for example, 'I like to drink milk; I have two brothers; I fell off my bike when I was five years old …'

Once they have finished the rest of the group can try to guess who is being described.

What Am I?

One player begins by thinking of an object and gives a clue by saying, for example, 'I am a light'. Now everyone else has to try and find out what kind of light they are by asking 'Yes'/'No' questions. If the answer to their question is 'Yes', they can ask another until they guess the answer or receive a 'No' answer, in which case someone else has a turn.

Example

'I am a light.'

☀ Are you normally inside a room? – Yes.

☀ Are you there all year around? – No.

☀ So you are only around during certain times of the year? – Yes.

☀ Are you a Christmas tree light? – Yes.

Suggestions

Shoe; song; building; drink; flower; tree; animal; planet; instrument, piece of furniture; road; piece of jewellery; weather.

Symbols

Everyday life is full of symbols: many businesses have well-known logos, there are recognisable signs everywhere and there are even symbols inside our homes, for example, rings, crosses and flowers.

Discuss the different sorts of symbols that we come across in everyday life, and then give the group some time to think about familiar symbols.

Now everyone can join in a group art project. Place a large piece of paper in the middle of the table along with a selection of paints.

Now everyone can paint the symbols they have thought of, these might include symbols that they don't necessarily like.

Once the painting is complete each person can choose one symbol they like and one they dislike and explain the reasons for their choices to the rest of the group.

What's My Mime?

Each person can take it in turns to perform a mime for the rest of the group.

To make the activity more fun, you could give the group themes to be acted out, or the group could be divided in two and group mimes performed for the other group to try and guess.

Mime Themes

☼ Occupations

☼ Shopping for different items

☼ Telephone conversations

☼ Animals

28

Tall Tales

This game requires time for preparation.

Give everyone a pen and paper and ask them to find a quiet space where they can write their own tall tale, including a number of false or contradictory statements.

Afterwards, players can take it in turns to read out their story and the other players have to try to spot as many false statements as possible.

Example

One lovely spring day I travelled with some friends to the New Forest. We all enjoyed the beautiful scenery and the scent of the moss in the forest. The leaves on the trees were turning red and orange. On our way back home, we drove past fields of wheat and sweetcorn where the seedlings were just beginning to show. Then we stopped and picked apples from a tree in a garden.

(Leaves only turn red and orange in the autumn and there are no apples on the trees in spring.)

No 'L'

This game is quite tricky, but can also be great fun.

The group must make up a story, one sentence at a time around the circle. However, there is a catch - they are not allowed to use words containing the letter 'L'!

Example

Player 1: 'One day up in the high mountains…'
Player 2: '… there resided some tiny dwarfs.'
Player 3: 'They occupied tiny stone huts.'

And so on, until every player has had at least one turn. If anyone breaks the rule they are out.

Variations

☼ Players are not allowed to use words containing double letters.

☼ Players are not allowed to use words that have fewer than three (four/five) letters.

☼ All the words in a sentence have to start with the same letter.

Scrambled Words

This game could be played by individuals or in teams.

Prepare some sheets for the group listing a selection of animal and bird names whose letters have been mixed up. The group members have to try and unscramble the words to find the solutions.

To make the task a little easier you can announce the themes in advance.

Examples

Enlgnhtigia	nightingale
Tealehnp	elephant
Emosu	mouse
Rabdeg	badger
Wolalws	swallow
Licertarpla	caterpillar
Doockpredew	woodpecker
Rifafeg	giraffe
Sorhe	horse
Bribat	rabbit

Spoon Game

Ask the group to sit in a circle and tell them that they must copy just what you do, or they will be out. How many people will get it right?

Hold a spoon in your left hand and use it to carry out an action, for example, tapping the table twice before passing it on to person on your right. This person must copy the action before passing the spoon on to the next player, who must do the same, and so on around the circle.

Does anyone manage to copy exactly your actions?

The trick

Before passing the spoon to the next player, you must pass it from your left to your right hand. Most people don't do this, but instead simply pass on the object using the hand that is already holding it.

A Sure Bet

This is a game for two players. Place 30 matches on the table. Players then take it in turns to take away up to six matches at a time. The player who takes away the last match is the winner.

How do you ensure that you always get the last match and win?

Solution

You must try to keep the number of matches left on the table divisible by 7.

If you are the person to start, take away two matches. This leaves 28 matches and 28 can be divided by 7. Thereafter, ensure that the total number of matches taken away by you and your partner always equals seven.

If your partner starts, you will have to work to try and use the 'can be divided by 7' rule to your advantage.

This can become very tricky if your partner starts by taking away two matches – do they already know the trick?

The Emperor Dislikes

Start by telling the group that they are going to have to listen carefully and work out what the emperor likes and dislikes.

The emperor likes snoozing, but not sleeping, milk but not orange juice, cola but not coke, a woman but not women, a child but not children, flying but not aeroplanes, and so on.

Using this information, players must try to work out what sorts of things the emperor doesn't like. Some people will find this quite difficult.

The solution

The emperor does not like anything that contains the letter 'e'.

Variations

To begin with choose single letters. Once the group is familiar with this game, you could make it more difficult by using words containing double letters or digraphs (oe, oo, ow, etc.). For example, the emperor likes to sleep, but doesn't like pillows.

The Last Question

Choose one member of the group to leave the room and wait outside, while everyone else sits together in a circle.

Now call the person back in. They must ask each player a question, one at a time around the circle. They can only ask each person one question and once they have received an answer they must move on.

The questioner has to try and work out why the other players are giving the seemingly strange answers. They can be assured that all questions are being answered truthfully and that they are more likely to work out what's going on if they ask questions requiring more than a 'yes'/'no' answer.

For example, they might begin by asking: 'Charlie, why is your hair so long?' The first answer will be: 'If only I knew.' The next question is: 'Clara, what kind of books do you like to read?' Answer: 'Because my head gets cold really quickly!'

Solution

From the second player onwards people are answering the previous person's question.

/... continued

Variation: Ship load

When the person re-enters the room they are told that the group will be loading a ship, and they must work out why the items are being chosen.

Each player names two items they would like to put on the ship. Sophie Long starts and chooses sausages and lentils.

Solution

Each item must begin with the initial letters of a person's first and last name. Alternatively, the solution could be the last letters in players' names.

Distraction Artists

Arrange three chairs in a triangle facing each other. One person is chosen to sit in each chair.

Person A starts by asking person C a question, for instance a simple sum. While they are speaking, person B starts to make slow movements with their arms or hands, for example, drawing a shape in the air. Person C has the most tricky task, because they have to try to answer the question while at the same time copying B's movements.

Start this game with an easy action, before gradually making both the question and the action more difficult.

Once all three people have had a turn, they can have a rest and watch three other 'distraction artists' performing.

Which member of the group is the best at performing two tasks at once?

Card Tricks

Card tricks can be fun – and difficult to work out. Here is one to baffle the group – see if anyone can work out how it is done.

Do any of the group members know tricks of their own?

First of all, shuffle the cards well. You could ask someone in the audience to do this.

Then take the deck of cards and make sure you memorise the card at the bottom of the deck without anyone noticing. Place the deck on the table and carry out some seemingly random shuffling, but make sure you keep an eye on where the bottom card is.

Ask a member of the audience to take a card and give it to you without looking at it themselves. Tell them the name of the card you memorised right at the beginning and place the card face down on the table.

Then ask the person to draw another card and tell them the name of the one they gave you previously, before also placing it face down on the table.

Finally, announce that you are going to choose the last card yourself, and that you will guess what it is. Choose the card that you have been keeping an eye on, and place it face down with the other two without looking at it.

Now name the second card the person from the audience gave you.

Quickly gather up the three cards and show them to the audience – you have named them all all correctly!

The Dynamic Square

Give each member of the group a sheet on which you have drawn a square consisting of three by three spaces.

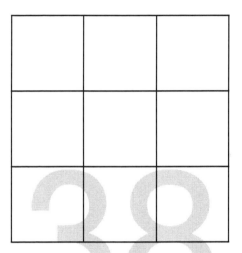

Using the numbers 1 to 9, they must write one number in each space making sure that the sum of the numbers in all three rows, all three columns and both diagonals adds up to 15. Give the group a set period of time to try and work it out, before giving clues one at a time if necessary.

/… continued

Clues

1 Write the number 5 in the middle space.
2 Write the number 8 in the bottom right space.
3 Write the number 2 in the top left space.

You are likely to be able to work out the rest yourself!

2	7	6
9	5	1
4	3	8

Polar Bear Game

Give the group some basic background information. In Greenland, polar bears predominantly live on fish, which they catch through holes in the ice. So in this game there can only be a polar bear where there is a hole in the ice.

Now roll three dice simultaneously and tell the group how many polar bears you can see.

Can they work out the solution?

Solution

There can only be polar bears when there is a hole in the ice. The holes are the dots in the middle of the dice.

For example, if a die shows a three, there is one hole with two polar bears. The four may show four polar bears, but there is no hole, so they are not counted. A five has one hole and four polar bears.

Add up the numbers of bears on the three dice and tell the players how many there are.

One = one hole, no bears
Two = no hole, no bears
Three = one hole, two bears
Four = no hole, no bears
Five = one hole, four bears
Six = no hole, no bears

The Detective

This is a good game for a long rainy afternoon.

The group are going to solve a mystery. You will need some of them to act the roles of the characters in the story. These include the criminal, the criminal's accomplices, victim(s) of the crime, the witnesses and the detective.

The list of characters can be extended, if necessary, depending on the size of the group.

Explain the rules to everyone before starting the game.

Choose who is going to be the detective, this person must now leave the room for a brief period of time. Now the others can agree on which character they want to be and the crime that has been committed. Then call the detective back in and tell them about the case (for example, a kidnapping or a hit-and-run).

The detective now starts interviewing everyone. The detective is only allowed to ask 'yes'/'no' questions. The players being questioned must answer truthfully based on the agreed story. Each person being questioned is allowed to refuse to answer three times in order to either try to mislead the detective or to direct suspicion towards someone else.

The detective has to try and find out who committed the crime, but is not allowed to ask someone directly whether they are the criminal. This requires a lot of skill as well as the ability to combine lots of information, which can become quite exciting.

You may want to consider limiting question time or awarding a prize to the detective if they can solve the crime.

Matchbox Nose

This is a lovely old game, which works particularly well when the group are relaxed and comfortable in each other's company. It can be played as one large group, or in smaller teams.

You will need the outer cases of matchboxes – as many as you have teams.

The teams must line up in the middle of the room. The first player starts by sticking the outside of a matchbox on to their nose and must try to pass it on to the next person's nose without anyone using their hands.

The first team to get the matchbox to the end of the line are the winners.

If anyone uses their hands or if the matchbox falls to the floor the team must start again.

Card Pile-Up

This game requires a minimum of eight players who should sit on chairs in a circle. Depending on the number of players or the level of difficulty you want to introduce, this game can be played using either card colours or suits.

Shuffle a pack of cards and then deal one card to each player.

Each person should memorise the colour (or suit) of the card they have been dealt before you collect all the cards back in again and shuffle them with the rest of the deck.

Now turn over one card at a time, calling out the colour/ suit of the card as you do so. Anyone whose chosen card was that colour must move around the circle, one place to their left. However, if the chair they are moving to is already taken, the player moving places has to sit on the other person's lap. Sometimes this can lead to two or even three people sitting on top of each other on the same chair.

If a player is sitting in the middle or at the bottom of a 'pile' and their colour is called out they are not allowed to move – only players at the top can move.

If the card turned over is a nine, the top and bottom people on any chair containing more than one player must swap places and the person who is now sitting on top is allowed to move on one place.

The winner is the first person to return to their original chair.

Hands & Feet

This is a good ice-breaker for new groups but can also be used at the end of term to see how well everyone knows each other.

Take a photograph of each person as they arrive. Let them think these are for a group portrait – but make sure you take the photograph in such a way that only a small part of each person can be seen, for example, a hand, a shoe, their bag, their hair and so on.

Once you have all the photographs the group can play the big picture guessing game. Print the pictures and put them on the wall or display them on a computer or television screen.

Give everyone a numbered answer sheet and ask them to try and work out who is in each picture.

How well do the group know each other?

Gordian Knot

This game works best with a maximum of twelve players.

Ask the group to stand in a wide circle. Now they must close their eyes, stretch out their arms and slowly walk towards the middle of the circle. Keeping their eyes shut, they must to try to find another hand to hold on to with each of their own.

Once everyone has linked up with two other hands, they can open their eyes. Now they have to try to un-knot themselves without letting go.

This is not always possible. If no solution can be found, the group can repeat the game and try again.

44

Hiding in the Dark

A great game for a large building or room – and is best played at night, although you can switch off the lights on a winter's afternoon.

No lights are allowed for this game – only the group leader is allowed a torch. Make sure any dangerous objects are moved before starting and check that no-one else in the building will be disturbed by the game.

Choose one or two people who must hide somewhere in the room or building. Give them a five-minute head-start. Then the search can begin. Anyone finding the two hidden players should keep as quiet as possible and, without attracting any attention, hide with them.

Eventually, the whole group will end up sitting together in complete darkness – trying not to giggle or make a noise!

This, of course, is the perfect setting for telling ghost stories by torchlight.

Pulse

Your pulse rate mirrors the activity of your heart. Ask the group to find their pulses and see how many heart beats they can count in a minute.

The object is for group members to find someone else whose heart beat matches their own.

Playing this game requires a quiet and unrushed atmosphere as well as an element of intuition. People should try and guess who might have the same heart rate as themselves and then approach that person and count their pulse.

They should keep doing this until they have found a person who has the same pulse rate. It is possible that three or more people find that they have the same pulse rate or even that some people may not find someone who matches them.

As the game progresses do people's heart rates change?

Note

☼ The best way to feel someone's pulse is to place two or three fingers on the inside of their wrist just below the root of the thumb.

☼ You should never use your thumb to feel someone else's pulse, as the thumb has a pulse of its own.

☼ The pulse rate for a healthy adult is between 60 to 80 beats per minute.

Birthday Line Up

This is a good game for groups who are new to each other.

You will need a minimum of six players, who do not know each other very well. Their task is to organise themselves into a line in order of age from youngest to oldest. Players are not allowed to talk while doing this and must only communicate using gesture. They need to take into consideration not just the year of their birth, but also the month and day they were born.

For example: Sam is standing on the far left, because his birthday is on 18 June 1985. Next to him is Nita, because she was born on 20 July 1985, and so on.

Once everyone has lined up, players can start talking to each other again to check whether their attempts at non-verbal communication have been successful and make corrections if necessary.

Where are You?

Two players are blindfolded and stand opposite each other at a distance of approximately 10 metres. At a signal, the blindfolded pair start walking towards each other with the aim of meeting in the middle.

The rest of the group stand around them, watching quietly as the two people cautiously approach and try to find each other.

Afterwards, give the players an opportunity to express the feelings, thoughts and maybe even fears they experienced during the game.

What senses did they use to find each other?

Then two other players can have a turn.

Ghost Game

This game needs a minimum of ten players and can be played with large groups depending on the space available. In addition, the game requires absolute darkness and can be played either in a large darkened room or outside at night.

Turn off the lights and ask the group to walk around quietly and slowly. One person is going to be chosen to play the role of the ghost. This can be done by the leader walking around and lightly touching someone on the shoulders.

If a player meets someone else as they are walking around, they must quietly whisper 'Ghost?' If there is no reply, this means that the person is not the ghost. However, if they have met the ghost, the ghost will respond by whispering 'Ghost' back.

When someone finds the ghost, they turn into a ghost themselves and should link arms or hold hands with the original ghost. The two ghosts now continue to walk around the room and if another player bumps into one of the ghosts, they also link up. This way, the ghost chain will become longer and longer with players linking onto the chain at both ends.

The game continues until the whole group has turned into one 'Big Ghost'.

Riding Waves

This game of trust requires a minimum of thirteen players.

The group lie down on the floor, making a 'zig-zag pattern': in diagonal pairs head to head with one person stretching their legs to the right, the other to the left and touching the feet of the next person, keeping close together. Now all players reach up their arms, palms facing upwards, to create a 'bed' or wave track.

One player stiffens their whole body and lies back (ideally helped by two others) onto the start of the wave track. It is important that they keep their body really stiff and their hands close to their body. The people making up the wave track then start using their hands to transport the person gently to the other end, where two people help them get off the track again. Players can take turns to be carried by the wave.

As with all games of trust, participation should be voluntary and the group needs to get on well.

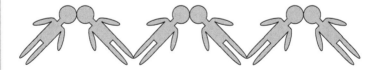

The 50 Best Games series ...

☼ These handy pocket books will ensure you are never again stuck for activity ideas that will help make both teaching and learning fun!

☼ Carefully selected, each collection of the 50 Best Games is themed and addresses a specific area of development. All the games are easy to implement with the minimum of preparation and can be adapted to the needs of your particular group.

☼ Use them as warm-ups, ice breakers, time fillers or to address a specific need. Suitable for groups of all sizes and can be used with all ages from young children to adolescents.

The 50 Best Games for Building Self-Esteem

ISBN 978-0-906531-18-8

The 50 Best Games for Sensory Perception

ISBN 978-0-906531-11-9

The 50 Best Games for Brain Exercise

ISBN 978-0-906531-14-0

The 50 Best Games for Relaxation & Concentration

ISBN 978-0-906531-17-1

The 50 Best Games for Speech & Language Development

ISBN 978-0-906531-13-3

The 50 Best Games for Children's Groups

ISBN 978-0-906531-12-6

The 50 Best Games for Groups

ISBN 978-0-906531-16-4

The 50 Best Indoor Games for Groups

ISBN 978-0-906531-15-7

Hinton House Publishers Ltd
Newman House, 4 High Street, Buckingham, MK18 1NT, UK
info@hintonpublishers.com
www.hintonpublishers.com

Have you seen ...

3 Minute Motivators

More Than 120 Activities to Help you Reach, Teach and Achieve!

Kathy Paterson

This resource will show you how to turn around unmotivated, unfocused classes. With more than 120 practical and simple ideas that will refocus a group, release excess energy, or start a class with a bang.

Offering a wide variety of ready-to-use activities that turn potential problems into opportunities, and get pupils out of a rut and into a more productive mode:

- *Calm Down* – relaxing activities that let imaginations soar
- *Get Moving* – lively motivators
- *Act, Don't Speak* – silent but fun activities
- *Words and Movement* – activities that mix talk with action
- *Single Words & Sounds* – simple communication activities
- *Conversation* – getting motivated one-on-one
- *Brainstorms* – working together to let the ideas fly
- *Paper & pencil activities* – from letter and word play to shared stories.

An ideal resource for all teachers, teaching assistants and those running groups, promoting playful activities that involve competition, cooperation and opportunities to focus on real learning.

2009 • 168pp • A4 paperback • ISBN 978-1-906531-00-3

Hinton House Publishers Ltd
Newman House, 4 High Street, Buckingham, MK18 1NT, UK
info@hintonpublishers.com
www.hintonpublishers.com